Ravette London

This edition first published by
Ravette Limited 1986

Printed and bound in Great Britain
for Ravette Limited,
12 Star Road, Partridge Green,
Horsham, Sussex RH13 8RA
by William Clowes Limited, Beccles and London.

ISBN 0 948456 14 0

How can you resist this lovable, adorable, cute example of 'felinity'. The wide-eyed smile, the cute button nose, those delicate features, and of course the warm hearted personality? Then of course there's Garfield..!

I THINK IT'S TIME YOU MET A LADY CAT, GARFIELD
JIM DAVIS
12-15
AND IF YOU'RE NOT SURE WHAT TO DO ON A DATE JUST WATCH ME IN ACTION SOMETIME
I HAVE
MAKE AN INNUENDO, GET SLAPPED. MAKE A SUGGESTION, GET SLAPPED. MAKE A MOVE, GET SLAPPED
© 1980 United Feature Syndicate, Inc.
JON SAYS THIS AFTER SHAVE IS SUPPOSED TO ATTRACT WOMEN
12-16
JIM DAVIS
GALLOP
GALLOP
GALLOP
GALLOP
DARN... WRONG SPECIES
© 1980 United Feature Syndicate, Inc.

IT'S TIME I MET A CAT OF THE FEMALE PERSUASION
JIM DAVIS
12-17
WHAT TOOK YOU SO LONG?
© 1980 United Feature Syndicate, Inc.
WHAT DO THEY CALL YOU?
12-18
JIM DAVIS
MY NAME'S ARLENE
AND WHAT DO THEY CALL THAT SPACE BETWEEN YOUR FRONT TEETH?
THIS RELATIONSHIP IS OFF TO A TENUOUS START
© 1980 United Feature Syndicate, Inc.

JIM DAVIS
12-19
WANNA EAT MICE?
WANNA BEAT UP DOGS?
HOW BARBARIC
HOW NAUSEATING
© 1980 United Feature Syndicate, Inc.
TELL ME, ARLENE, WHAT GOOD IS THAT SPACE BETWEEN YOUR TEETH?
JIM DAVIS
12-20
WHEN WILL I SEE YOU AGAIN?
NEXT TIME I WANT TO HAIL A TAXI
© 1980 United Feature Syndicate, Inc.

HEY, GARFIELD. NERMAL'S COME TO VISIT FOR THE WEEK
10-13
I WISH I COULD KEEP HIM
KITTENS ARE LIKE STRINGS... EVERY YO-YO WANTS ONE
© 1980 United Feature Syndicate, Inc.
JIM DAVIS
AWWWWW, ISN'T NERMAL CUTE?
10-14
LOOK KID... JON IS **MY** OWNER. THIS IS **MY** TERRITORY. **I'M** THE CUTE ONE AROUND HERE. GOT IT?
IT'S EASIER TO CHARM YOUR WAY THROUGH LIFE IF YOU HAVE THE MUSCLE TO BACK IT UP
JIM DAVIS
© 1980 United Feature Syndicate, Inc.

I HATE NERMAL. I THINK I'LL CLEAN HIS CLOCK
10-15
HEY, KID. HOW'D YOU LIKE TO PLAY ON THIS WAFFLE IRON?
BUG OFF
I GUESS I'LL HAVE TO USE MORE SUBTLE MEANS
© 1980 United Feature Syndicate, Inc.
JIM DAVIS
10-17
KICK!
© 1980 United Feature Syndicate, Inc.
WHERE DID NERMAL GO?
HE'S TAKING A SHORT NAP
JIM DAVIS

CLOP
CLOP
JIM DAVIS
HA HA, CATS ARE SO CUTE WHEN THEY PLAY DRESS-UP
CUTE TO A POINT, THAT IS
10-18
I HAVE A TABBY AT HOME JUST LIKE YOU
6-27
HEE-HEE. AREN'T YOU CUTE!
WHERE ARE YOU GOING, GARFIELD?
TO PUT A RUNNER IN THAT LADY'S SUPPORT HOSE
JIM DAVIS

TOMORROW I'LL BE TWO YEARS OF AGE. THAT'S THE HUMAN EQUIVALENT OF FOURTEEN
6-18
CATS HAVE IT GOOD
ADOLESCENCE WITHOUT ACNE
JIM DAVIS
© 1980 United Feature Syndicate, Inc.
TODAY IS MY BIRTHDAY, AND I HATE BIRTHDAYS. I'M GOING TO GET A SURPRISE PARTY, AND I HATE SURPRISE PARTIES
JIM DAVIS
© 1980 United Feature Syndicate, Inc.
SURPRISE, GARFIELD!
BUT I **LOOOOOVE** THE ATTENTION!
6-19

HOW ABOUT DINNER TONIGHT, DOC?
SURE
IF THERE'S NOTHING GOOD ON TELEVISION
DID YOU HEAR THAT, GARFIELD? SHE PRACTICALLY THREW HERSELF AT ME!
PRAY FOR RERUNS, HOTSHOT
9-29
JIM DAVIS
JUST ONCE I'D LIKE TO GO ON A DATE WITHOUT GARFIELD
JIM DAVIS
WHERE TO, SIR?
9-30

THIS IS AN EXCLUSIVE RESTAURANT, GARFIELD. THEY'LL NEVER SERVE A CAT HERE
© 1980 United Feature Syndicate, Inc.
WEAR THIS
JIM DAVIS 10-1
NOW SIT UP STRAIGHT... SON
WAIT'LL WE GET HOME... DAD
GOOD EVENING, LIZ. SO GLAD YOU COULD JOIN US
© 1980 United Feature Syndicate, Inc.
10-2
"US"?
ME AND MY CAT
YOU'RE NOT STRANGE OR SOMETHING ARE YOU?
YOU DON'T KNOW THE HALF OF IT, LADY
JIM DAVIS

HA HA HA, WHEEEE!
POW!
WHEN WAS THE LAST TIME YOU HAD SO MUCH FUN, GARFIELD?
I THINK IT WAS THE TIME I GOT THE HAIRBALL STUCK IN MY THROAT
JIM DAVIS
10-3
© 1980 United Feature Syndicate, Inc.
THANKS FOR A LOVELY EVENING, LIZ
KISS
10-4
© 1980 United Feature Syndicate, Inc.
PTOOY PTOOY
YOU LUCKY DOG. I RARELY KISS ON THE FIRST DATE
JIM DAVIS

CATS ARE NOT ONLY CUTE AND FUZZY...
WE ALSO MAKE KEEN ALARM CLOCKS
AT NO EXTRA CHARGE
JIM DAVIS
© 1980 United Feature Syndicate, Inc.
10-11
GARFIELD, I WISH YOU WOULDN'T KEEP BURYING ODIE IN THE SAND
BIG DEAL
I ONLY BURIED HIM UP TO HIS KNEES
8-14
© 1980 United Feature Syndicate, Inc.
JIM DAVIS

THE MOON IS RIGHT
4-20
JIM DAVIS
THE TIME IS RIGHT
© 1980 United Feature Syndicate, Inc.
GOOD EVENING, LADIES AND GERMS. A FUNNY THING HAPPENED ON THE WAY HERE TONIGHT...
A CANARY WALKS UP TO ME THE OTHER DAY AND HE SAYS, "I HAVEN'T HAD A BITE IN THREE DAYS." SO YOU KNOW WHAT I DID?
JIM DAVIS
4-21
I ATE HIM!
© 1980 United Feature Syndicate, Inc.
YAH DAH DAH DAH DAH DAH
TAPPITY TAPPITY TAPPITY

O SOLO
♫MEYOW♪
JIM DAVIS
4-22
© 1980 United Feature Syndicate, Inc.
I KNOW YOU'RE OUT THERE. I CAN HEAR YOU BREATHING
TAKE MY DOG... PLEASE
JIM DAVIS
4-25
WHAT'S THAT?
© 1980 United Feature Syndicate, Inc.
HOOK!

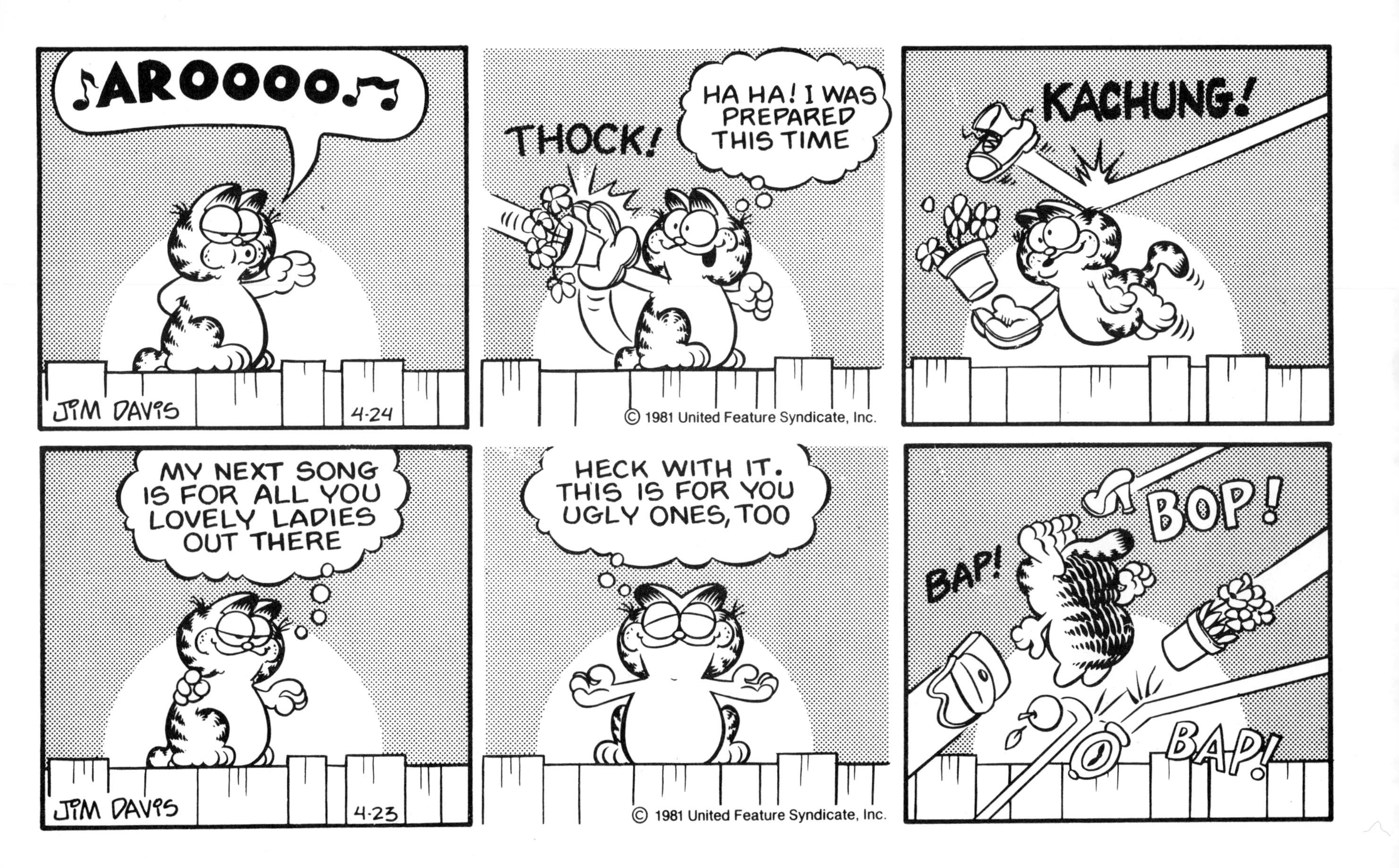
AROOOO.
JIM DAVIS
4-24
THOCK!
HA HA! I WAS PREPARED THIS TIME
© 1981 United Feature Syndicate, Inc.
KACHUNG!
MY NEXT SONG IS FOR ALL YOU LOVELY LADIES OUT THERE
JIM DAVIS
4-23
HECK WITH IT. THIS IS FOR YOU UGLY ONES, TOO
© 1981 United Feature Syndicate, Inc.
BAP!
BOP!
BAP!

HERE I AM, NERMAL, THE WORLD'S CUTEST KITTEN!
JIM DAVIS
11-30
WHAT MAKES YOU THINK YOU'RE SO CUTE?
SIMPLE, **ALL** KITTENS ARE CUTE UNTIL THEY GROW INTO CATS AND BECOME UGLY
I DIDN'T HAVE TO HEAR THAT
I TELL IT LIKE IT IS, BABY CAKES
© 1981 United Feature Syndicate, Inc.
I WONDER HOW NERMAL CAN STAY SO CUTE AFTER ALL THESE YEARS?
12-1
JIM DAVIS
PAT
PAT
PAT
I THOUGHT SO
MUD PACK
© 1981 United Feature Syndicate, Inc.

FOLD
FOLD
JIM DAVIS
12-2
CAN I PLAY TOO?
SURE... GRAB HOLD
© 1981 United Feature Syndicate, Inc.
SLEEP ON MY TEDDY BEAR, WILL YOU?!
Z
JIM DAVIS
12-3
Z
I WISH I COULD DO THAT
Z
© 1981 United Feature Syndicate, Inc.

GARFIELD, I GET THE IMPRESSION YOU DON'T LIKE NERMAL
NONSENSE. I LOVE NERMAL
I JUST LOOOVE NERMAL!
UH... UH, GARFIELD
JIM DAVIS 12-4
© 1981 United Feature Syndicate, Inc.
HEY, NERMAL, WANNA RACE TO THE FRONT DOOR?
YOU WIN
SLAM
12-5 JIM DAVIS
© 1981 United Feature Syndicate, Inc.

YOU AGAIN
ME AGAIN
6-1
JIM DAVIS
NERMAL, THE WORLD'S CUTEST KITTEN
NOW, STAND ASIDE, FATSO. I HAVE PEOPLE TO CHARM
© 1981 United Feature Syndicate, Inc.
OUT!
JIM DAVIS
6-2
YOU CAN SCRATCH MY CHAIR, YOU CAN INSULT MY MOTHER, YOU CAN BEAT UP MY DOG, AND YOU CAN PLAY WITH MY RUBBER MOUSIE...
© 1981 United Feature Syndicate, Inc.
BUT YOU DON'T EAT MY FOOD AND YOU DON'T SLEEP IN MY BED
YES, SIR

WE CATS ARE VERY INDEPENDENT
JIM DAVIS
6-3
WE DON'T NEED ATTENTION
UNLESS IT'S BEING GIVEN TO SOMEONE ELSE
© 1981 United Feature Syndicate, Inc.
COME HERE, NERMAL
6-4
MAKE YOURSELF USEFUL
JIM DAVIS
WHERE ARE YOU GOING?
TROLLING FOR DOGS
© 1981 United Feature Syndicate, Inc.

6-5
JIM DAVIS
MINE!
POOKY IS A ONE-CAT TEDDY BEAR
© 1981 United Feature Syndicate, Inc.
I GUESS I'LL BE LEAVING
MUST YOU RUSH?
JIM DAVIS
IF YOU INSIST, I'LL STAY
© 1981 United Feature Syndicate, Inc.
6-6

BOP!
6-12
JIM DAVIS
WHANGO
NOBODY BEATS UP ON ODIE BUT ME
© 1981 United Feature Syndicate, Inc.
DO YOU KNOW WHAT I HATE ABOUT DOGS?
JIM DAVIS
6-13
DOGS ARE ... SO ... SO
FRIENDLY
© 1981 United Feature Syndicate, Inc.

CHRISTMAS SPIRIT...
12-25
JIM DAVIS
IT'S NOT THE GIVING. IT'S NOT THE RECEIVING
IT'S THE LOVING. MERRY CHRISTMAS
© 1981 United Feature Syndicate, Inc.
WHAT A NICE CHRISTMAS. I GOT AN EYE FOR MY TEDDY BEAR, SAND FOR MY SANDBOX, AND A NEW BLANKET
12-26
JIM DAVIS
THIS IS WHAT HAPPINESS IS ALL ABOUT...
© 1981 United Feature Syndicate, Inc.
SECURITY

LOOKING GOOD, GARFIELD
YOU STILL HAVE IT, YOU RASCAL
AN ACTIVE IMAGINATION IS A WONDERFUL THING
JIM DAVIS
12-12
© 1981 United Feature Syndicate, Inc.
IT IS KIND OF PRETTY OUT HERE ON THE FARM
CHIRP CHIRP
WALT DISNEY, EAT YOUR HEART OUT
4-4
JIM DAVIS
© 1981 United Feature Syndicate, Inc.

TONIGHT I AM GOING TO TAKE LIZ OUT **SOLO**. YOU ARE STAYING HOME, GARFIELD
JIM DAVIS
12-17
WHERE'S MY FAVORITE TIE?
© 1981 United Feature Syndicate, Inc.
I GET TO GO WITH YOU, AND THE TIE LIVES
WHAT SAY WE DOUBLE DATE, OLD BUDDY?
GOOD EVENING, LIZ. I HAVE A WONDERFUL TIME PLANNED FOR US
JIM DAVIS 12-18
© 1981 United Feature Syndicate, Inc.
WE'LL HAVE DINNER, GO TO A MOVIE, AND MANY MORE THINGS TOO NUMEROUS TO MENTION
YOU BROUGHT THE CAT
THAT WAS ONE OF THE UNMENTIONABLES

THANK YOU FOR A LOVELY DATE, JON
JIM DAVIS
KISS
12-19
© 1981 United Feature Syndicate, Inc.
YAH TAH TAH TAH, YAH TAH TAH TAH
HUMAN LOVE... IT'S SO GLANDULAR
CLICK
POOR ME... STUCK UP A TREE
JIM DAVIS
7-9
THINGS COULD BE WORSE, I GUESS
© 1981 United Feature Syndicate, Inc.

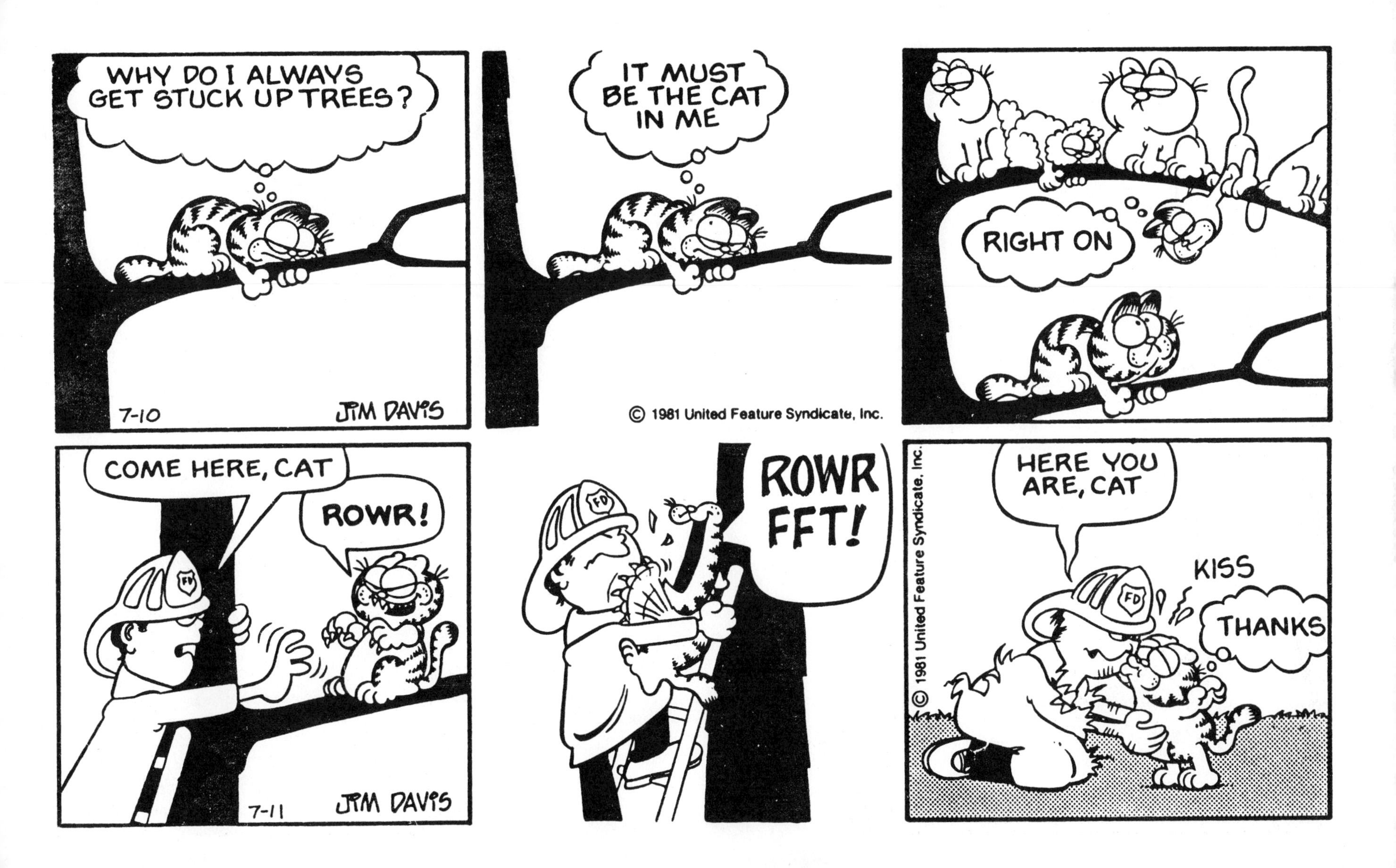
WHY DO I ALWAYS GET STUCK UP TREES?
7-10
JIM DAVIS
IT MUST BE THE CAT IN ME
© 1981 United Feature Syndicate, Inc.
RIGHT ON
COME HERE, CAT
ROWR!
7-11
JIM DAVIS
ROWR FFT!
© 1981 United Feature Syndicate, Inc.
HERE YOU ARE, CAT
KISS
THANKS

JIM DAVIS
5-28
© 1981 United Feature Syndicate, Inc.
JIM DAVIS
TELL ME THAT'S NOT A TRAFFIC COP'S HAT YOU'RE WEARING, GARFIELD
OKAY, IT'S NOT A TRAFFIC COP'S HAT
5-29
© 1981 United Feature Syndicate, Inc.

I'M BORED. I THINK I'LL STEP OUT FOR SOME FRESH AIR
JIM DAVIS
5-30
GARFIELD! WE ARE GOING OVER 50!
SO I NOTICED
© 1981 United Feature Syndicate, Inc.
WHY WERE CATS PLACED UPON THIS EARTH?
4-27
JIM DAVIS
WHY, TO GIVE PEOPLE PLEASURE
© 1981 United Feature Syndicate, Inc.
AND TO GIVE DOGS A HARD WAY TO GO
SMACK!

BOING
BOING
JIM DAVIS
HA HA, AREN'T YOU CUTE! HERE, HAVE SOME FOOD
1-4-82
I HATE MYSELF WHEN I DO THAT
© 1981 United Feature Syndicate, Inc.
WHAT SAY WE GO FIND SOMETHING TO EAT?
IS THAT ALL YOU THINK ABOUT-FOOD?
4-13
© 1982 United Feature Syndicate, Inc.
OF COURSE NOT, MY LOVE...
JIM DAVIS
THIS BUSINESS OF SLEEPING HOLDS A GREAT DEAL OF FASCINATION FOR ME
A REAL RENAISSANCE MAN

FOOD, FOOD, FOOD, IS THAT ALL YOU THINK ABOUT, GARFIELD?
THAT'S ABOUT IT
4-14
© 1982 United Feature Syndicate, Inc.
SO WHAT AM I, CHOPPED LIVER?
JIM DAVIS
DON'T FLATTER YOURSELF
HE CERTAINLY KNOWS HOW TO MAKE A GIRL FEEL GOOD
DO YOU KNOW WHAT I LIKE ABOUT WOMEN?
JIM DAVIS
4-15
THEY ARE SO SOFT
COME TO THINK OF IT...
© 1982 United Feature Syndicate, Inc.

© 1982 United Feature Syndicate, Inc.

JIM DAVIS 7-7
AREN'T YOU CUTE
ROWR!
© 1982 United Feature Syndicate, Inc.
WHY, YOU VICIOUS BRUTE!
WHAT HAPPENED TO "CUTE"?
I WISH JON WOULD GET MARRIED
JIM DAVIS 7-10
FWEEE
THE ONLY WAY HE KNOWS MY DINNER IS READY, IS WHEN IT SETS OFF THE SMOKE ALARM
© 1982 United Feature Syndicate, Inc.

I GOT YOU A NEW FRIEND, GARFIELD. HE EVEN TALKS
OH, GOODY
JIM DAVIS
10-6
WILL YOU PLAY WITH ME?
WHY, OF COURSE, LITTLE BUDDY
LET'S GO PLAY WITH JON'S POWER TOOLS
© 1982 United Feature Syndicate, Inc.
I WONDER WHAT THIS BAG OF SAWDUST HAS TO SAY
JIM DAVIS
10-7
FEED ME FEED ME FEED ME FEED ME FEED ME
© 1982 United Feature Syndicate, Inc.
HE DOES HAVE A CERTAIN CHARM

IMAGINE, THE NERVE OF JON GIVING ME A DUMMY AS A COMPANION. WHAT KIND OF AN INTELLECTUAL DWARF DOES HE THINK I AM?
JIM DAVIS
10-8
PRACTICE OF THE ARISTOTELIAN MEAN WOULD HAVE A SIGNIFICANT POSITIVE EFFECT ON THE WORLD INSTITUTIONAL ENVIRONMENT
© 1982 United Feature Syndicate, Inc.
OH, SHUT UP
YOUR LITTLE FRIEND HERE IS CERTAINLY CUTE, GARFIELD
JIM DAVIS
10-9
STOMP!
STOMP!
STOMP!
LITTLE FRIEND OR NOT, THERE'S SOMETHING TO BE SAID FOR THE DIPLOMATIC REMOVAL OF COMPETITION
© 1982 United Feature Syndicate, Inc.

GOOD MORNING, GARFIELD. IS THERE SOMETHING YOU'RE TRYING TO TELL ME?
JIM DAVIS
12-20
IT'S THE CHRISTMAS SEASON, YOU SAY
© 1982 United Feature Syndicate, Inc.
GIMME, GIMME, GIMME, GIMME, GIMME, GIMME, GIMME, GIMME
JIM DAVIS
12-21
GIMME! GIMME! GIMME! GIMME! GIMME! GIMME!
I'M GETTING INTO THE CHRISTMAS SPIRIT
© 1982 United Feature Syndicate, Inc.

JIM DAVIS
12-22
THAT'S GOTTA BE A WORLD'S RECORD!
THE PRESENTS GO THERE. MOVE IT, MOVE IT, MOVE IT
© 1982 United Feature Syndicate, Inc.
I HOPE THIS GIFT IS MINE
RATTLE
RATTLE
RATTLE
JIM DAVIS
CRACK!
TINKLE
TINKLE
TINKLE
12-23
I HOPE IT'S ODIE'S
© 1982 United Feature Syndicate, Inc.

IT'S ONLY NOON, GARFIELD. ARE YOU GOING TO BED ALREADY?
THE SOONER YOU GO TO BED, THE SOONER IT'S CHRISTMAS MORNING
JIM DAVIS
12-24
GOOD NIGHT, LITTLE FELLA
COMICS READERS ARE VERY SPECIAL PEOPLE. YOU MEAN MORE TO ME THAN THERE IS SPACE HERE TO EXPRESS
I LOVE YOU ALL
HAVE A HAPPY HOLIDAY. I'LL BE FUNNY AGAIN TOMORROW, TRUST ME
JIM DAVIS
12-25

ROWR
JIM DAVIS
3-22
© 1982 United Feature Syndicate, Inc.
BOOT
AND NOW FOR THE MAIN ATTRACTION
TESTING, ONE, TWO. TESTING, ONE, TWO
ROWR
3-23
© 1982 United Feature Syndicate, Inc.
CAN YOU HEAR ME THERE IN THE BACK?
GOOD
JIM DAVIS

I LOVE SHOW BUSINESS. GIMME THE FULL MOON. GIMME THE FENCE
3-24
© 1982 United Feature Syndicate, Inc.
KAWHOCK!
GIMME THE BROKEN TEETH. GIMME THE MULTIPLE LACERATIONS
JIM DAVIS
'CAUSE MOMMA WAS A GREAT OLD GALLLL
♫MROOW♪
3-25
© 1982 United Feature Syndicate, Inc.
THANK YOU FOR THAT LARGE ROUND OF INDIFFERENCE
JIM DAVIS

WHAT'S THE DIFFERENCE BETWEEN A DOG AND AN EGGPLANT?
JIM DAVIS
3-26
© 1982 United Feature Syndicate, Inc.
ABOUT THREE IQ POINTS
BAP!
BOP!
BOOP!
JIM DAVIS
TAPPITY
TAPPITY
TAPPITY
3-27
© 1982 United Feature Syndicate, Inc.
OKAY... WHO WAXED THE FENCH?

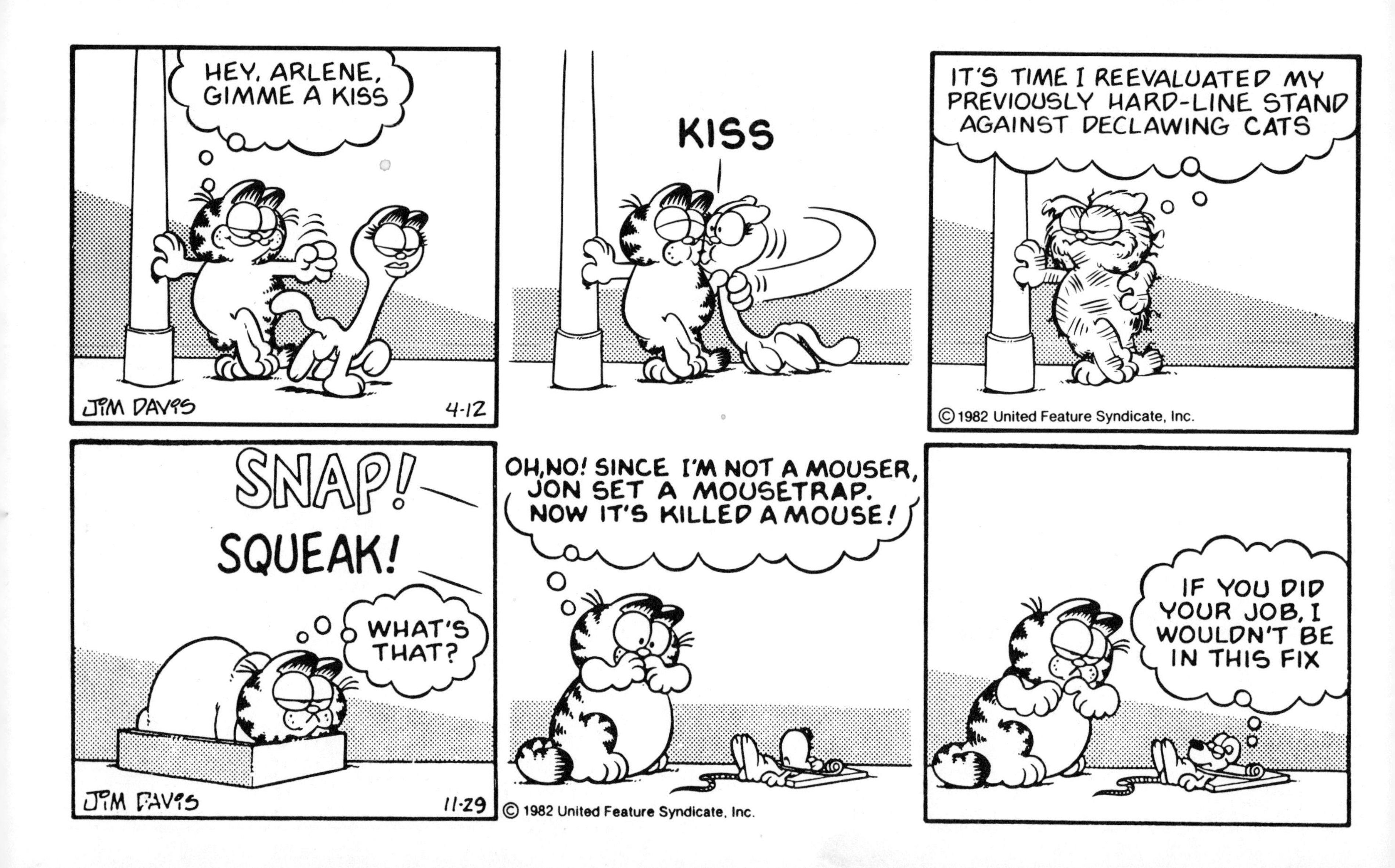
HEY, ARLENE, GIMME A KISS
JIM DAVIS
4-12
KISS
IT'S TIME I REEVALUATED MY PREVIOUSLY HARD-LINE STAND AGAINST DECLAWING CATS
© 1982 United Feature Syndicate, Inc.
SNAP!
SQUEAK!
WHAT'S THAT?
JIM DAVIS
11-29
OH, NO! SINCE I'M NOT A MOUSER, JON SET A MOUSETRAP. NOW IT'S KILLED A MOUSE!
© 1982 United Feature Syndicate, Inc.
IF YOU DID YOUR JOB, I WOULDN'T BE IN THIS FIX

I'M SORRY YOU GOT CAUGHT IN THAT MOUSETRAP, MOUSE
OH, THAT'S OKAY. I HAVE A WIFE AND EIGHT KIDS
JIM DAVIS
11-30
WHAT DOES THAT HAVE TO DO WITH ANYTHING?
THIS IS THE FIRST PEACE AND QUIET I'VE HAD IN YEARS
© 1982 United Feature Syndicate, Inc.
HAVE A PIECE OF CHEESE, MOUSE. MAYBE THAT WILL MAKE YOU FEEL BETTER
JIM DAVIS
12-1
© 1982 United Feature Syndicate, Inc.
HOW AM I SUPPOSED TO SWALLOW?
GOOD POINT

YOU'RE FREE TO GO, MOUSE
THANKS
JIM DAVIS
JUST WHERE HAVE YOU BEEN? I SUPPOSE YOU AND YOUR FAT FRIEND HAVE BEEN HAVING FUN WHILE I'VE BEEN WORKING AND SLAVING TAKING CARE OF OUR CHILDREN. YOU'D BETTER GET YOURSELF HOME RIGHT NOW
© 1982 United Feature Syndicate, Inc.
SNAP!
12-2
NOW GET OUT OF HERE
© 1982 United Feature Syndicate, Inc.
SNAP!
SQUEAK!
JIM DAVIS
12-3

JON WILL BE CHECKING THIS TRAP SOON
© 1982 United Feature Syndicate, Inc.
MY BUNNY SLIPPERS?
THEY LIKE TO ROAM AT NIGHT
12-4
JIM DAVIS
JIM DAVIS
SPUT SPUT
WEEEEZE
GURGLE
SPUT
© 1982 United Feature Syndicate, Inc.
10-26
THE CAR HAS STOPPED AND IT'S GETTING DARK. WHAT SHOULD I DO, GARFIELD?
I CAN ONLY THINK OF ONE THING
MAKE IT GO!

WE'RE STRANDED, GARFIELD. WE'LL HAVE TO FIND SOMEWHERE TO SPEND THE NIGHT
JIM DAVIS
© 1982 United Feature Syndicate, Inc.
WHAT ABOUT THAT PLACE?
CUTE
10-27
A LITTLE PAINT, A FEW CURTAINS, AND IT WOULD BE A REGULAR LOVE NEST
DON'T KNOCK THOSE FLOWERS OFF THE WINDOWSILL, GARFIELD
I PUT THEM THERE TO GIVE THEM SOME SUN
JIM DAVIS
© 1982 United Feature Syndicate, Inc.
AND SOME FRESH AIR
12-6

WINDOWS ARE GREAT. THEY OFFER A FRONT ROW SEAT TO LIFE'S PASSING PARADE
JIM DAVIS 12·7
THUD!
© 1982 United Feature Syndicate, Inc.
THEY ARE ALSO GOOD FOR A YUK OR TWO
I SEE YOU'RE BRINGING THE MAIL IN WITH YOUR USUAL CARE
JIM DAVIS 12·8
THIS LETTER SAYS, "DO NOT FOLD, SPINDLE OR MUTILATE"
IT DIDN'T SAY ANYTHING ABOUT "MAUL"
© 1982 United Feature Syndicate, Inc.

JIM DAVIS
12-9
MY NEWSPAPER! YOU CHEWED UP MY NEWSPAPER!
IT'S THINGS LIKE THIS THAT MAKE ME WONDER IF YOU SHOULD BRING IN THE PAPER AT ALL
PRECISELY
POO
© 1982 United Feature Syndicate, Inc.
ON CHILLY MORNINGS, THIS IS MY FAVORITE PLACE IN THE WHOLE HOUSE
12-10
JIM DAVIS
OVER THE HEAT VENT
© 1982 United Feature Syndicate, Inc.

GARFIELD, DID YOU EAT MY FERN?
© 1982 United Feature Syndicate, Inc.
WHY IS IT I GET BLAMED FOR EVERYTHING AROUND HERE? IF SOMETHING GOES WRONG, YOU JUST LAY IT ON OL' GARFIELD!
12-11
JIM DAVIS
I HAVE NO IDEA WHAT YOU'RE TALKING ABOUT
WHAT SHOULD I DO TONIGHT?
1-6-83
JIM DAVIS
SPLUT
© 1982 United Feature Syndicate, Inc.
GOOD IDEA. I THINK I'LL GO SING ON THE FENCE

OH, NO! FIRE ARROWS!
THOCK
1-7-83
I'M A GONER!
THOCK
© 1982 United Feature Syndicate, Inc.
A CAT ALWAYS GOES DOWN WITH HIS FENCE!
JIM DAVIS
I CAN'T BELIEVE THAT TACKY PACK OF MUSIC HATERS BURNED MY FENCE DOWN
1-8-83
JIM DAVIS
THE ONLY THING TO DO IS TO GET RIGHT BACK UP THERE AND START SINGING AGAIN
© 1982 United Feature Syndicate, Inc.
BUT... SOMEHOW IT JUST ISN'T THE SAME

UH-OH! HERE COMES THAT MEAN DOG!
JIM DAVIS
11-26
NOBODY WOULD EVER HARM A SLEEPING CAT
WRONGO
© 1982 United Feature Syndicate, Inc.
I'M TAKING YOU TO A GREAT RESTAURANT TONIGHT, ARLENE
JIM DAVIS
5-27
BONK BONK
LOOK, GALVANIZED. NOT ONE OF THOSE CHEAP PLASTIC PLACES
NOW I'VE SEEN IT ALL... A THREE-STAR GARBAGE CAN
© 1983 United Feature Syndicate, Inc.

I'LL SEE YOU, ARLENE
IT IS CUSTOMARY, IN HUMAN CIRCLES, TO KISS A LADY'S HAND
YOU'RE NOT A HUMAN, AND THAT'S NOT A HAND. THAT'S A HAIRY PAW
OIL AND WATER, NITRO AND GLYCERIN, CHIVALRY AND REALISM
JIM DAVIS 5-28
© 1983 United Feature Syndicate, Inc.
THIS IS MY HUMBLE ABODE, MY DEAR
JIM DAVIS 1-20
© 1983 United Feature Syndicate, Inc.
WHO WERE THEY?
OH, JUST A COUPLE OF ANIMALS I'M GIVING AWAY SOON

GARFIELD, SOMETIMES I THINK YOU DON'T LIKE IT WHEN I HAVE DATES
ABSOLUTELY
JIM DAVIS
1-21
DATING LEADS TO MARRIAGE. MARRIAGE LEADS TO CHILDREN
AND DO YOU KNOW WHAT CHILDREN DO TO CATS?
© 1983 United Feature Syndicate, Inc.
I WONDER WHAT AWFUL THING IS GOING TO HAPPEN TO ME TODAY? MAYBE THE SKY WILL FALL. MAYBE ODIE WILL BRING HIS LONG LOST TWIN BROTHER HOME...
JIM DAVIS
2-7
OR WORSE YET, MAYBE NERMAL WILL COME FOR A VISIT
© 1983 United Feature Syndicate, Inc.

OH SURE, YOU'RE GETTING ALL THE ATTENTION RIGHT NOW, NERMAL. BUT WHEN YOU GROW UP YOU'LL BE AS UNLOVED AS I AM
JIM DAVIS
2-8
I'M NEVER GROWING UP
WHO ARE YOU? PETER PAN OR SOMETHING?
I'M A MIDGET
SOME CATS GET ALL THE LUCK
© 1983 United Feature Syndicate, Inc.
IF YOU WANT TO BE CUTE LIKE ME, YOU HAVE TO PLAY WITH A BALL OF YARN
THAT SOUNDS SIMPLE ENOUGH
JIM DAVIS
2-9
YOURS IS OVER THERE
I HATE HIM
© 1983 United Feature Syndicate, Inc.

NERMAL, YOU'RE SO SWEET, WHY DON'T I JUST STUFF YOU INTO THIS SUGAR BOWL
JIM DAVIS
2-10
GO AHEAD AND TRY IT, FAT BOY
© 1983 United Feature Syndicate, Inc.
SAY, GARFIELD, WHERE'S NERMAL?
AT A HUMILITY LESSON
YOU DISGUST ME, NERMAL
JIM DAVIS
2-11
YOU'RE A WIDE-EYED, MINDLESS LITTLE PIECE OF FLUFF. YOU'RE SO CUTE EVERYONE LOVES YOU
EAT YOUR HEART OUT, BOZO
I AM, I AM
© 1983 United Feature Syndicate, Inc.

UNK
YOU'VE OVERSTAYED YOUR WELCOME
2-12
© 1983 United Feature Syndicate, Inc.
WHERE'S NERMAL?
YOU KNOW... IT WAS STRANGE, HE MUTTERED "UNK" AND THEN LEFT WITHOUT A WORD
JIM DAVIS
GIVE ME A KISS, SWEETHEART
JIM DAVIS
3-19
KISS
HOW DO YOU TELL A LADY HER MUSTACHE NEEDS MORE WAX?
© 1983 United Feature Syndicate, Inc.

HERE COMES ARLENE. SHE'S CRAZY ABOUT ME
JIM DAVIS
10-10
HI, ARLENE
I SAID... "HI, ARLENE"
© 1983 United Feature Syndicate, Inc.
HEY, ARLENE. GUESS HOW MUCH WEIGHT I CAN PRESS
JIM DAVIS
10-11
I'LL BET YOU DON'T KNOW
I'LL BET I DON'T CARE
RIGHT NOW I'D TRADE ALL THIS STRENGTH FOR JUST ONE SNAPPY COMEBACK
© 1983 United Feature Syndicate, Inc.

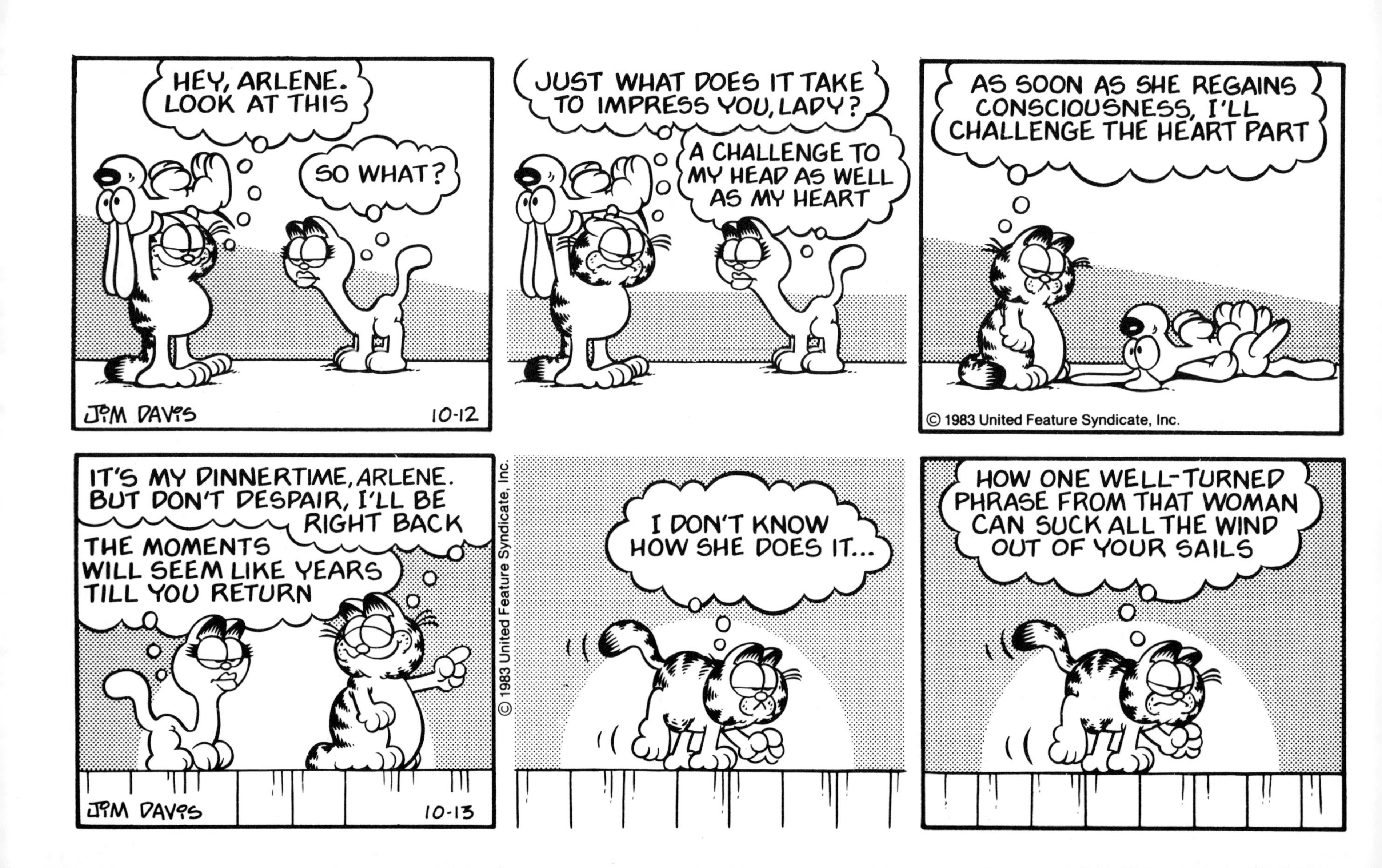
HEY, ARLENE. LOOK AT THIS
SO WHAT?
JUST WHAT DOES IT TAKE TO IMPRESS YOU, LADY?
A CHALLENGE TO MY HEAD AS WELL AS MY HEART
AS SOON AS SHE REGAINS CONSCIOUSNESS, I'LL CHALLENGE THE HEART PART
JIM DAVIS
10-12
© 1983 United Feature Syndicate, Inc.
IT'S MY DINNERTIME, ARLENE. BUT DON'T DESPAIR, I'LL BE RIGHT BACK
THE MOMENTS WILL SEEM LIKE YEARS TILL YOU RETURN
I DON'T KNOW HOW SHE DOES IT...
HOW ONE WELL-TURNED PHRASE FROM THAT WOMAN CAN SUCK ALL THE WIND OUT OF YOUR SAILS
JIM DAVIS
10-13
© 1983 United Feature Syndicate, Inc.

ARLENE, I'M SICK OF THE WIT-MATCHING MOOD YOU'RE IN
OKAY, I'LL STOP IT
THERE'S NO BATTLE OF THE INTELLECTS HERE ANYWAY
YOU'RE RIGHT. IT WAS KIND OF LIKE SWATTING A FLY WITH A BUICK
JIM DAVIS 10-14
© 1983 United Feature Syndicate, Inc.
HOW ABOUT A KISS, ARLENE?
WHAT KIND OF ANIMAL ARE YOU?
A CAT!
AUUGH!
I DID IT! I DID IT! SHE SAID, "WHAT KIND OF ANIMAL ARE YOU?" AND I SAID, "A CAT!"
JIM DAVIS 10-15
© 1983 United Feature Syndicate, Inc.

IT SEEMS LIKE AN AGE SINCE I GAVE ODIE A BOOT
JIM DAVIS
6-11
BOOT!
I'M JUST A SENTIMENTAL FOOL
© 1983 United Feature Syndicate, Inc.
POOKY!
JIM DAVIS
10-1
SO MUCH FOR KICKING THE TEDDY BEAR HABIT
IT'S UNNATURAL TO BE NEAR SOMEONE YOU LOVE AND NOT HOLD THEM NOW AND THEN
© 1983 United Feature Syndicate, Inc.

YOU DON'T LIKE ME, DO YOU?
I LIKE YOU
JIM DAVIS
NO, YOU DON'T
I'M CRAZY ABOUT YOU. I LOVE YOU
7-19
NOW WHY DON'T YOU GO PLAY IN THE BLENDER?
SEE?
© 1983 United Feature Syndicate, Inc.
WHY DON'T YOU LIKE ME?
YOU'RE YOUNG AND YOU'RE CUTE
JIM DAVIS
7-20
IF I WERE OLD AND UGLY, WOULD YOU LIKE ME?
POSSIBLY
WHERE'S MY CANE? WHERE'S MY CANE?
THIS MUST BE ONE OF THE THINGS CATS DO WHEN THEY THINK THERE ARE NO HUMANS AROUND
© 1983 United Feature Syndicate, Inc.

LOOK AT ALL THOSE PEOPLE. ALL GOING TO WORK TO PROCESS FOOD, PRODUCE ELECTRICITY, MANUFACTURE KITTY LITTER AND SO ON
ALL JUST FOR ME
I'D THANK THEM INDIVIDUALLY, BUT THEY KNOW WHO THEY ARE
JIM DAVIS 11-14
© 1983 United Feature Syndicate, Inc.
HERE COMES ARLENE. SHE'S CRAZY ABOUT ME
HI, ARLENE
HI, BOZO
I'M SURE SHE MEANT TO SAY, "HUNK"
JIM DAVIS 5-23
© 1983 United Feature Syndicate, Inc.

LET'S GO MOUSING
WHAT'S WRONG WITH LASAGNA?
THERE'S NO THRILL OF PURSUIT
OBVIOUSLY, YOU'VE NEVER SNATCHED ONE OFF THE TABLE DURING SUNDAY DINNER
JIM DAVIS
5-24
© 1983 United Feature Syndicate, Inc.
WHY DO GIRLS ALWAYS SMELL SO GOOD, ARLENE?
WE WEAR PERFUME
SOUNDS KIND OF SISSIFIED TO ME
I GET THIS FROM A SEX THAT LIKES TO TATTOO THEMSELVES
5-25
JIM DAVIS
© 1983 United Feature Syndicate, Inc.

WHAT DOES THE MOON REMIND YOU OF, GARFIELD?
5-26
THE MOON REMINDS ME OF NIGHT, AND THAT REMINDS ME OF SLEEP, WHICH REMINDS ME OF BREAKFAST...
JIM DAVIS
© 1983 United Feature Syndicate, Inc.
THAT WASN'T WHAT I HAD IN MIND
THEN, AFTER BREAKFAST, COMES MY NAP...
IT'S TIME YOU EARN YOUR KEEP AROUND HERE, GARFIELD. THERE'S A MOUSE HOLE AND THERE'S SOME CHEESE. YOU KNOW WHAT TO DO
JIM DAVIS
12-5
I CERTAINLY DO
© 1983 United Feature Syndicate, Inc.

HERE'S THE SCENARIO: CAT CROUCHES BY CHEESE WAITING FOR MOUSE TO EXIT HOLE TO RETRIEVE SAME. CAT CATCHES MOUSE. FADE OUT. THE END
JIM DAVIS
12-6
HECK WITH IT
© 1983 United Feature Syndicate, Inc.
I PREFER STORIES WITH A HAPPY ENDING
WHY SHOULD I HAVE TO CATCH AN INNOCENT LITTLE MOUSE? I HAVE NOTHING AGAINST HIM. IN FACT, HE'S KIND OF LOVABLE
JIM DAVIS
12-7
IF YOU DON'T CATCH THAT MOUSE, I'M PUTTING YOU OUT IN THE COLD!
THE FURRY TWERP DIES
© 1983 United Feature Syndicate, Inc.

THIS IS DEMEANING. I HAVE A NOBLE HERITAGE. I AM A UNIQUE, VITAL INDIVIDUAL
JIM DAVIS
12-8
AND ALL I'M CONSIDERED AS AROUND HERE IS A MOUSETRAP
© 1983 United Feature Syndicate, Inc.
I MUST SPEAK TO MY KITTY LITTER CHANGER ABOUT THAT
I DON'T WANT TO CATCH THIS MOUSE. HE'S CUTE. I'VE EVEN NICKNAMED HIM...
JIM DAVIS
12-9
© 1983 United Feature Syndicate, Inc.
"STRETCH"

JIM DAVIS
12-10
LIVE AND LET LIVE, I SAY
© 1983 United Feature Syndicate, Inc.
1-12
JIM DAVIS
GARFIELD, YOU SEEM TO BE PREOCCUPIED THIS WEEK
HUH?
© 1983 United Feature Syndicate, Inc.

OH, NO! DON'T MAKE ME DO IT! ANYTHING BUT THAT!
JIM DAVIS
TURN BACK! TURN BACK!
12-12
© 1983 United Feature Syndicate, Inc.
SOMETIMES, A CAT'S FEET JUST GOTTA CLIMB
HERE I AM, STUCK UP A TREE. THINGS COULDN'T BE WORSE
JIM DAVIS
12-13
OKAY, OKAY, NOW THINGS COULDN'T BE WORSE
© 1983 United Feature Syndicate, Inc.
BOOM

I MAY BE STRANDED UP A TREE...
JIM DAVIS
BUT AT LEAST I'M ON A STURDY LIMB
12-14
© 1983 United Feature Syndicate, Inc.
THE STORY OF MY LIFE
THIS ISN'T SAFE
JIM DAVIS
12-16
SHOO! SHOO! SOMEBODY MIGHT GET HURT!
© 1983 United Feature Syndicate, Inc.
TOING!

HEY, FATSO. WHAT DOES A BIRD LIKE YOU EAT?
JIM DAVIS
12-15
CATS
© 1983 United Feature Syndicate, Inc.
CHIRP CHIRP
A WAY DOWN! ALL I HAVE TO DO IS DIVE INTO THAT BIRDBATH
12-17
© 1983 United Feature Syndicate, Inc.
7.0
6.5
JIM DAVIS

I'M LONELY. I THINK I'LL SEE IF I CAN FIND ARLENE
JIM DAVIS
5-14
HI THERE
YOU TWO-TIMING SWINE!
© 1984 United Feature Syndicate, Inc.
WHAT HAPPENED?
HI, ARLENE
DON'T SPEAK TO ME, YOU CAD. I SAW YOU WITH THAT OTHER WOMAN!
5-15
JIM DAVIS
OH COME ON NOW, DO I LOOK LIKE THE KIND OF GUY WHO COULD EASILY ATTRACT WOMEN?
I SUPPOSE YOU'RE RIGHT
© 1984 United Feature Syndicate, Inc.
AND JUST WHAT DO YOU MEAN BY THAT?!

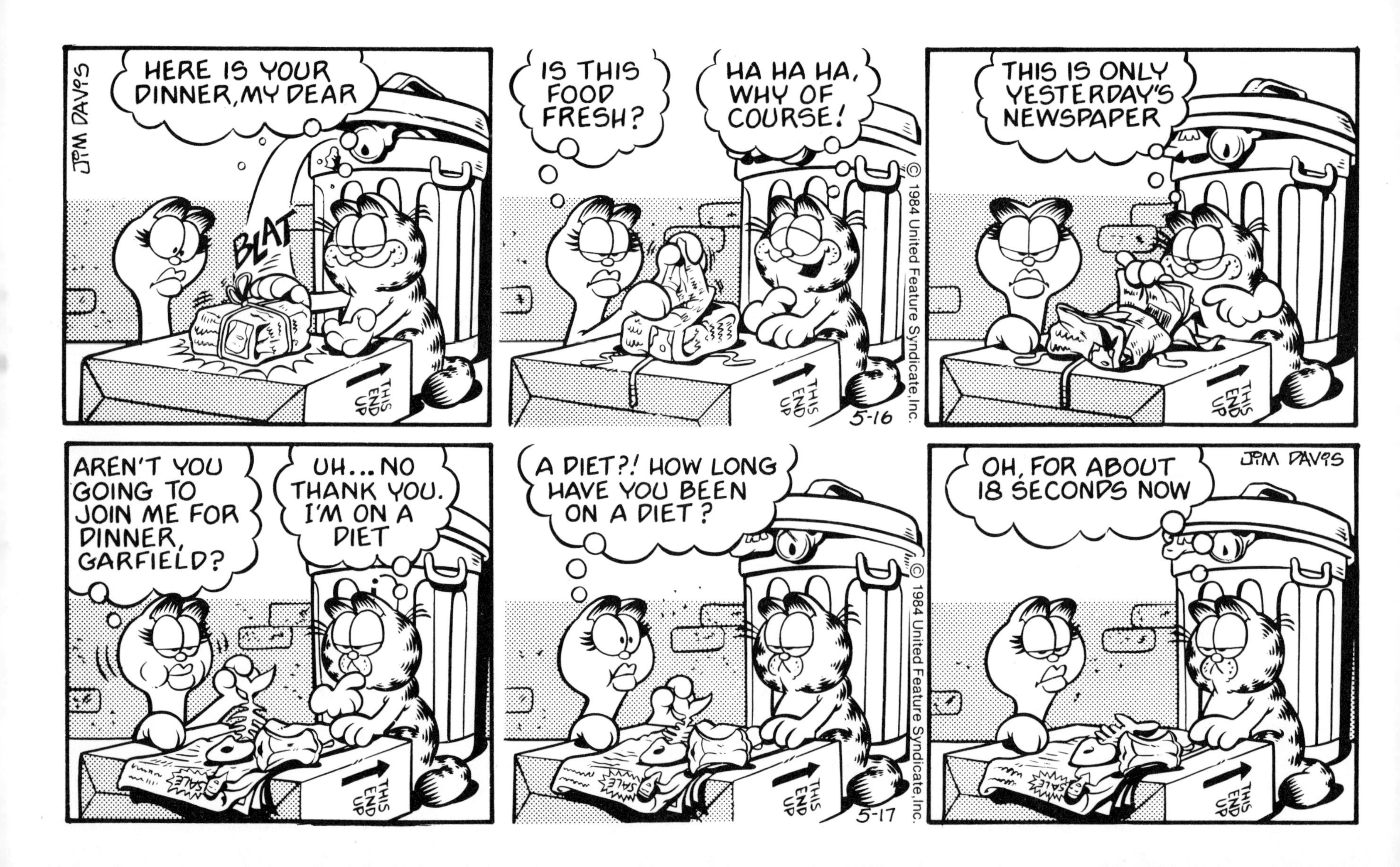
JIM DAVIS
HERE IS YOUR DINNER, MY DEAR
BLAT
IS THIS FOOD FRESH?
HA HA HA, WHY OF COURSE!
THIS IS ONLY YESTERDAY'S NEWSPAPER
THIS END UP
© 1984 United Feature Syndicate, Inc.
5-16
AREN'T YOU GOING TO JOIN ME FOR DINNER, GARFIELD?
UH... NO THANK YOU. I'M ON A DIET
A DIET?! HOW LONG HAVE YOU BEEN ON A DIET?
OH, FOR ABOUT 18 SECONDS NOW
JIM DAVIS
SALE
THIS END UP
© 1984 United Feature Syndicate, Inc.
5-17

HO HUM...
5-18
JIM DAVIS
WHY DO WE SEE EACH OTHER?
IT BEATS BEING LONELY
© 1984 United Feature Syndicate, Inc.
I WAS HOPING FOR SOMETHING MORE ROMANTIC
THAT'S WAY DOWN THE LIST
5-19
JIM DAVIS
IS OUR DATE OVER?
DID IT BEGIN?
© 1984 United Feature Syndicate, Inc.
SOME WOMEN DON'T APPRECIATE US STRONG, SILENT TYPES

GOOD MORNING, GARFIELD. IT'S ME, NERMAL. I'M YOUNG AND GOOD-LOOKING AND YOU'RE NOT
I DIDN'T NEED THAT
1-23
JIM DAVIS
© 1984 United Feature Syndicate, Inc.
CAN I GET YOU ANYTHING FOR BREAKFAST, GARFIELD?
YEAH, HOW ABOUT A BIG GLASS OF FRESHLY-SQUEEZED KITTEN JUICE?
YOU DON'T LIKE ME, DO YOU?
1-24
JIM DAVIS
© 1984 United Feature Syndicate, Inc.

HOW CUTE! NERMAL BROUGHT ME MY NEWSPAPER
JIM DAVIS
1-25
AND MY SLIPPERS AND MY PIPE! WHAT MORE COULD A MAN WANT?
HOW ABOUT A WOMAN?
© 1984 United Feature Syndicate,Inc.
GOOD EVENING, LADIES AND GERMS. I'D LIKE YOU TO MEET POOKY, MY GAG WRITER
JIM DAVIS
7-5
SPLAT
© 1984 United Feature Syndicate,Inc.
WELCOME TO SHOW BIZ, KID

POOKY LOVES ME. I CAN TELL
7-3
JIM DAVIS
HE DOESN'T TALK, HE DOESN'T WALK, HE DOESN'T THINK
A LITTLE NOTHING GOES A LONG WAY
© 1984 United Feature Syndicate, Inc.
I'M WORKING UP A ROUTINE FOR THE FENCE TONIGHT, POOKY. TELL ME WHAT YOU THINK OF IT
JIM DAVIS
7-4
I KNEW A TEDDY BEAR WHO WAS SO UGLY, EVEN THE TIDE WOULDN'T TAKE IT OUT
© 1984 United Feature Syndicate, Inc.
BLAT!

LET'S GET YOU INTO TROUBLE, NERMAL
1-26
JIM DAVIS
LOOK IN THE COOKIE JAR! LOOK IN THE COOKIE JAR!
NO, YOU CAN'T HAVE A COOKIE, GARFIELD. YOU'LL SPOIL DINNER
© 1984 United Feature Syndicate, Inc.
THANKS FOR THE COOKIES
JEFF WOULD HAVE KNOWN WHAT LASSIE WAS TALKING ABOUT
ODIE
JIM DAVIS
1-27
BLUT! BLUT!
ODIE
© 1984 United Feature Syndicate, Inc.
CALL IT CRUEL. CALL IT JUVENILE. I CALL IT ASSERTING MYSELF
ODIE

I HATE TO BOTHER YOU, SIR, BUT YOU PUT INSUFFICIENT POSTAGE ON YOUR PACKAGE
© 1984 United Feature Syndicate, Inc.
WHAT PACKAGE?
THIS KITTEN YOU'RE SENDING TO ABU DHABI
GARFIELD
JIM DAVIS 1-28
IT'S MONDAY OUT THERE. I FEEL IT IN THE AIR. I HATE MONDAYS
I'M SURE THE WORLD WILL END ON A MONDAY... AT LEAST I HOPE IT DOES
IT WOULD BE A SHAME TO END THE WORLD RIGHT BEFORE A WEEKEND
JIM DAVIS 4-2
© 1984 United Feature Syndicate, Inc.